One Dance

George Bishop

FUTURECYCLE PRESS
www.futurecycle.org

Library of Congress Control Number: 2016953787

Published by FutureCycle Press
Lexington, Kentucky, USA

ISBN 978-1-942371-17-5

For Chris Meyers

Contents

4

"A truth ceases to be true
when more than one person believes it"
—Oscar Wilde

"Whatever satisfies the soul is truth"
—Walt Whitman

1

Calling

Somewhere sort of sacred inside
I'm an abandoned rural church

darkened by figures of stained
glass that broke into me at birth.

I'm the young priest who died
years ago, his secrets still filling

the empty pews with an incense
of nights alone, confessions kept

to himself rising to a bell tower
where there's never been a bell.

Late at night he lights the candles
of himself, counts the plates

passed to no one, pauses as if
forgiveness had said something.

The originals of a god are long lost
in the dead sea of his back pocket,

messages beginning and ending
in the broken rib of his belief.

Downed Lines

All those connections cut off by
a rabid pack of gusts, lightning

let loose like an experiment gone
wrong, maybe a gang of unknown

gods with nothing better to do
than insist we're alone for awhile

to strengthen their existence. You
have to believe in something deep

in the country when the road's out
and wires are snapping at the asphalt,

toying with our pathetic attempts
at prophecy. We're all thinking of

the last thing we said, how it will
always mean something else.

Roads

Shadowed in the early hours, a late spring
morning begins to surface, just something
we can't explain at first, the same answers.
Appetites step out of the cedars, disobey
some small evolutionary footnote—fear

tiptoes over the instinct a deer has set aside.
The dark knows what it's doing, stays close
enough to the stars, closer to the moon, sets
the usual dares adrift in the air. I'm doing
85 down the hollow of this highway tonight,

not one intuitive muscle moving in me,
a different kind of hunger already feeding
out in the open of my impatience. Our faces
pass at the speed of death, survival arriving
too late. Nothing happens. Our shadows

come crawling back. Codes of color join
hands with each escape as they slow down,
carefully covering the fresh trails of dead
ends. The signs were all there. The signs
are always there, shadowed in early hours.

Headlights

It could be a drunk, a cop, someone
so familiar with exits they don't need

a sign, they just take one. Maybe it's
me behind the headlights, going home

alone to be alone where other headlights
are coming at me all the way to sleep

and beyond. There's a tug, darkness—
the black pines box me between stars

and cracking tar. Trust's heartless half
has passed, the part I never trusted

and always will. It's turning around.
It always does. I can feel it—the heat

hidden deep in the eyes of brake lights,
skid marks measuring my uncertainty,

knowing a part of me always refuses to
pull over on nights like these—almost

somewhere, identification all hit and run,
a little truth in the eyes of every alias.

Return Address

homeless at Biscayne Bay

One by one they appear, punctual
as any junior executive—less coffee,
alternatives, the instincts of a postman.
They gather by the bay to stare out
the day before, unsigned self portraits,
each one so brushed over by a blank
bloodshot narrative they can't keep it
to themselves, the surface of every eye
empty except for the sun's memos—

revise and revise. What kind of signature
signs them in each day—first name, last?
Only death knows our last and our first
will lead us there in a blur of duplicates
so compromised by what we're not, one
by one we'll open as the homeless have
appeared—pushing what's always been
empty, stage names and loose change
sharing the same hole in separate pockets.

Dog Homeless and Down

Cities seemed to suit me best, something homeless
hanging in every eye, the windows of the unspoken

painted shut and endless alleys of unexplored
silence—makes you wonder what sleep is made of

on nights of anybody, anywhere, anytime. However,
homeless in a hometown puzzles familiar ghosts,

family pushing you from one dead member to another,
until the smell of your first name (and only your first)

has drifted out of town, your home town. Same silence,
just a different past in your future. Loneliness only

goes so far before it turns back, but distance will never
desert you, no blood above the door of your old bed-

room, no street life that passes for life. It was so far
from my mind, this distance—I've begun to love it,

its longing, the timeless desires to undress, the steady
release of what's in between the hard sleep of shelters.

The Wrong Hotel

I was still thinking someone slept poorly
here the night before as I pulled the bed

sheets back, still dreaming of new ways
to keep from dreaming. In my drinking

days I would've spoken to everything,
keeping my good eye on the present as it

sat somewhere in the room staring at itself
like a dead star. I've never been able to wish

on anything other than that, so here I am
surrounded by the afterglow of stale tobacco

and bad booze, sleepless. I think I'll stay
another night, maybe see what the maid is

made of—after all, the desk clerk threw me
the keys like I'd been here before, same floor,

same stairs, just the wrong hotel, different
night, someone checking out inside as if

the light of sleep hadn't reached him yet
from the dreams of all his empty rooms.

Along Orange Blossom Trail

A skeleton of scaffolding between billboards
had become home to an osprey, a huge nest

hidden behind two colorful ads, plenty of room
to pick apart fish, fill a few holes with bone.

The young will love it when they come, spacious
enough for the newborns to feel fresh blood

finding its way to a pair of untested wings.
I keep it all to myself, gull-like, unable to tell

the difference between the taste of trash
and the aroma of a life just lived—my appetite

has taught me to share only what I drop,
reminding me I'm not very good at what I do.

Trails

So she could cope with the guilt
she renamed the dog before taking it
to the pound—which got me thinking
about guilt and how I've shaken it

most of my life, lost it on some false
trail I fashioned. It wasn't easy being
rescued all those times, forgiving
the home in homeless and naming

the streets just off the streets. I found
real self pity needs strong family ties
and accountability can only be felt
by something thick and hidden like

a wallet. I told her it wasn't even
necessary to forgive herself, guilt
is part of a good home, sometimes
all there is that can pick up a scent.

Proposals at East Lake

Pink and baby blue splashed lake-sky, the air
so still you could hear gators getting final

instructions before heading out of their holes
for a half-moon evening of prehistoric stalking

and flash-snaps too quick for the eye—light
and dark are all that play by the rules out on

East Lake (anywhere, actually) this far south.
The whole peninsula hatches more change

than marriage on a good night, sun-drenched,
blistering blacktop burning off so much rain...

like the blizzard of...
                          up north where home fires

twist stories and crack their whips at disbelief.
Sure is pretty, though—going down, falling

off, coming up somewhere else. Like marriage
on a bad day, you have to know how to read

the water and swim against the stars. Edges
are always calling out when the air is still as...

One Failure Away

The black cat in me camps on the edge
of something, always ready to run down

a desire, his good eye fixed on temptation
trolling the fixed heart of hunger. However,

he's come back barely a cat too many times,
been fooled by taste half his and half mine.

We both know we're better at windows,
more alive with what shatters holding us

back, the silence of a glass field filling us.
We're only one failure away. Just one.

2

Salt Love

to a passenger

Like an empty ferry slip
late at night—that opening,

creosote feathering loose
lines in air older than love,

salt stinging in the shallows
of her stare anymore, that

stoic after-face of faith healed
of memory, dead at the edge

of herself. She's waited long
enough, then a little more.

She's the night of us all,
steady, on schedule, her heart

always a beat behind saving
what's sinking in her eyes.

Opening Panacea

Two nights ago—Panacea and its Christmas
parade of boats, a tree lighting and little girl

finding carols with one finger. I couldn't find
one complicated moment, not one question for

the part of me that questions all celebrations.
Tiny lights lit up every vessel, looking worthy

of the sea inside each captain towing them,
sirens at each end, Santa out there practicing

Yes and *Yes*. This year Miss Wakulla County's
long, black hair has me wrapping gifts for my-

self I'll never open. I couldn't live like this.
I'm too used to surviving peace, tending

the wounds of getting too close. Sometimes
it's good to be a stranger, the kind of present

that's easy to open and wrap again, to save
for your solitude. I feel at home. Somewhere.

Sleeping With Rips

They tell us never to resist, go with it
until the release is another thing beyond
your control. You're out where you can't
touch, holding on to water as tight as you can,
when you notice your weakness has given away
too much and you're sure something knows
what to do. You're where you watched gulls
attack with such abandon that you're convinced
the only hope is to try to forget what's next—

swim parallel to the beach, then to shore, try
not to think of passengers thrashing against
the deadened insistence of gravity, their ship
broken apart, settling. But you think of them
as you feel something let go. Stories begin
to surface. You're dragging them up on
the sand—you can't resist, even though
your legs have been missing since you fell
asleep one night in the net of a hammock.

Waking Up Asleep

to my sister

That dream you told me
about, the one where dolphins
tugged at your bedsheets—
I've been diving for meanings
ever since, holding my breath
below the surface of answers
that appear and disappear
as the hours ocean over night.
Bathing in this troubled back-
water only darkens it, drags me
around what's happened as it
happens again another way.

Perhaps something's gone down
you don't know about—wrecks
like this can't all be uncovered.
Your visions have searched me,
discovered the lost channels
my sleep sails from. They ride
my wake to what sank slowly
deep inside and came to a rest
just out of reach. It appears to be
the dream you told me about,
the one where dolphins
tugged at your bedsheets.

At Oyster Point

Low tide. Marsh. The oyster
beds made dark and twisted.

The rats love it, though; fits
their thoughts. A few of mine

have stood up, taken notice—
yesterday, when love had gone

all the way out, I found what
I lost grown together, perfect

combinations casting spells,
pearls ducking every one. But

it's always possible shallow
marshes like mine are wild

with things you can't see. Like
Oyster Point digging through

itself, my soul's feet are cut
and black, the gem I promised

myself hidden somewhere
in sleep. I've tracked blood

all the way home some nights—
I've followed something back.

Bald Point

You're told over and over by the bayou
behind you that this is where winter winters,

that your footprints are meaningless, going
nowhere. You hope for a shell of something

because every few feet you want to stop
and pull yourself up into some dark past,

relive the best parts. Finally a dead man-
o'-war speaks, but it's just you—you with

all the names nothing answers to, nothing
you can hear from the end of Bald Point.

Impatient at Diana's Salon

for Diana

The man with no hair was next, or maybe
I couldn't see what he considered out of place,

something only certain mirrors might recognize.
I couldn't find one overrun ear on the others

in line; every edge was razor-sharp. They came
for something else, I decided, a cut out of reach

for clippers, too knotted for combs to groom.
They were back for a touch of Diana's double,

a woman's reflection working on their own.
They've wanted it for weeks; the rich glow

of cologne said so. They take a deep breath
as she gently presses the paper tunic in place,

adjusts the chair, begins. She wants them
to keep only enough to desire more, to dizzy

them with an interest just a few movements
short of caring. They need to believe they'll

look different when they come back. I can't
describe the way I feel when it's my turn—

no gray growing in my eyes, just falling to
the floor as I forget what I wanted to say.

It passes so quickly you think it will never end.
Busy? I ask, moving myself to another mirror.

Night Light

before the affair

I'm thinking yacht—sails
pulled, kicker and tide

dead even. Commotion down
the beach—a fisherman struggling

with what's gone deep, alone
like a good fisherman should be,

close to his lies. I turn the light
to a party boat, blood on the deck,

no chance for fish stories here,
too many things getting away—

the perfect mount, make it
a skin mount, scales still full

of the last moon. Next morning
it's all buoy and glassy seas

warning me where not to go
after I've gone, reminding me

of home—the porch light, stories
I pushed overboard before bed.

Housebreaking Love

The wildness of first meeting, lust
landing almost immediately, its only eye
shut, speed reduced to slurs, the greed
of laughing gulls caught in its throat.
The barren beach of living alone
slowly moved offshore, island-driven,
no place to survive, where I survived.
Inside I'm still crawling out of some
sea, the invisibility of a life below
a surface barely visible now. In a land
of alarms, timers and porch lights,
the urge to get away, like any urge,
is all I know of eternity, even though
I keep insisting there's more. Lust
says so, the original home fire we pen
home by, reaching all the way to wet
sand, wildness and first meeting.

Vacation Cottage

It was a rental. No heat. On bad days
everyone would sit in different rooms

and watch it rain, whether it was raining
or not. When we spoke again our voices

would fill the hollow walls behind unsigned
oils of something somewhere else. Come

January the lights were out, windows
shuttered. We wrote for years, but

the cottages began to disappear in winter.
They had no heat and some of us wanted

to stay. That's when things were insulated
and our summer secrets turned to lies.

One Dance

For two sandhill cranes that's all it took,
a silly one, too, I suppose, on the lake—

maybe a few young males hanging back,
shifting their legs to a beat so natural

it couldn't be heard. It was all heart;
there wouldn't be another. Weeks later

I watched an alligator stalking an adult
and its colt, swimming the shoreline in

perfect prehistoric harmony with the pair.
When the cranes came to the end of the trail

there was nowhere else to go; the crane
began to peck at its offspring with a long,

lethal beak until it was dead, then pushed
off into the air to find its mate. The one.

Cheating

Bullet holes waiting
for what's alive
in the air—too much
time in a stranger's
eyes, all the way in.
And even though you'll
never see her again,
she'll be back. Next morning
you spin your barrel
of thoughts, ready yourself
for the cock and aim
of her lover in you.
She hides behind him;
you step in her shadow—
We can't miss. We miss.
Or we don't. It's always
there, alive in the air.

Stone

at her grave

Her husband turned to the afterlife when
something incurable found a way to him.
He prepared for things that soon might go on
somewhere beyond his body—even bought
two plots, hoping his wife would one day
join him. And after he passed, she arrived

at the cemetery each day, ready to seed
the loose, dark earth with prayer—engaging
in her own funerals over the vacancy at
his side—until the soil where they'd sleep
forever was washed into every empty answer.
There's a churchyard in us all we keep tended,

wicks we light, angels we purchase to polish
the grounds of our past, other days digging
to a smooth surface. *Until we meet again,*
their stone says. It's a date, the unsigned end
signing some new romance she can't refuse.
There are things that won't wash away even

if they wash away, and it's hard to turn down
a heaven the love of your life has left you,
to give away the gift of a grave. Sometimes
it's pure hell waiting for a name—wondering
who you'll meet again, when you meet again,
and what was cured, if it matters. Sometimes.

A Stranger Sits Across From Me
Taking the Last Chair in the Cafeteria

She appeared. Japanese. Skin white
as ivory. It all sounded like a flower

blooming as she gestured toward
the only empty seat left in the hall.

I wanted to touch her the way a child
instinctively wants to touch a doll

or a gun, always depending on how
much sex has been stirred since

birth. Four smiles separated everything
there was about her from what little

I knew of myself. She painted herself
in and out of my life like a day lying

down on a hidden lake, then withdrawing
to a star—nothing left but light.

3

Still Life With Recipes

Sitting in one of my favorite restaurants,
facing the mural of a 1950s fair, I silently
spoke to the children again as they waved
to one other—him leaning into the horse
of a carousel, her about to descend
into a dark and dry tunnel of love—both
imagining a finish line I couldn't see. It
wasn't long before I began to wander the art
of my own childhood, everything won, lost,
worthless tokens spread out in my eyes like
dead stars. It seemed life had taken a turn,

become my own private house of mirrors,
aging secrets everywhere, a kissing booth
with no way out and out of order. The key
to a safe I thought was safe has unlocked
itself, slipped the combinations of my past
behind the crystal ball buried somewhere
deep in the fairgrounds. Dessert arrives—
French silk pie because I love the name,
how it reminds me of a fortune waiting
for someone else on a clean, white canvas,
the artist arriving out of his own still life.

Lightning and Love

(Lakeside)

There are dogs shivering uncontrollably
beneath beds made of more complicated

love. They've mastered the art of begging,
live in the shadows of this late summer,

the humid air wearing away instinct after
instinct. It gets ugly in the grass after a dry

spell: nitrogen's of no use, cicada sounds
rip through the trees as roots get edgy and thin.

Horizons are thick and gray with warnings,
the sky hurling thunder as far as it can until

it becomes no more than some barrier
broken—an apple against the earth,

a book finding its way back to a shelf—
too much, too close, too long.

Some Shapes at Dusk

Two bats no more blind than
a pair of doves bounce off
their own radar, part butterfly,
all hunt. Love bugs black
and tasteless beg to die beside
their eggs, their only day over-
grown with sex and acidic bore—
no bite, no sting. Sound shadows
draw near; my illusory affairs
with doubt empty into sketch-
books of chance, survival.
Just before dark, the light
of being alone is like waking
up in a small town named after
another small town far away,
maps of yourself you don't own
opened, and searching alleys.

Shelling

Oyster beds bearing no resemblance
to anything desirable, where I'd love
to nap, dream or die—the abandon
of pelicans and ruin of shells wears
away in every wave. Everything
pieced, worn, hidden, regret growing
just below the skin of an old man
nose to nose with another old man,

telling him off, telling it like it is—

maybe the chiseled frowns of women
tobacco-bound, carved into mirrors
that mistake them for the dark cracks
in a wall they can't detect. Whatever
it is I'm looking for, this is as close
as I can come—a colander of shells
soaking in dish soap and warm water,
the inside of emptiness coming clean.

Designing Mirrors

to my love

Never thought I'd find you there, edging yourself
with shells, working each worn shape into a broken

harbor, your serious side centered, flowered with
half emptiness and designs of survival that didn't

survive, even in mirrors where things feel unbreakable.
You add a shard of sea glass, a heart-shaped cut

of coquina, oyster bouquets and a perfectly vacant
lettered olive—something to listen to as you fuss with

a lock of hair, a smile, a promise. Maybe, because
a conch can't be half of anything, the way in is the way

out, like a mirror, always looking back, as it oceans over
what can only be partially found, barely believed.

Writing in the Sand of Myself

It's what I didn't pass on that goes on.
Summer nights sea-bound and sand-crazy,

words loose as slippers, tight as a sailor
can tie a knot onshore. I say anything,

I mean everything. I don't notice tides.
One day I notice a full moon coming up

from the end of October and something
goes back, but not me. I'm spinning

away, sailing the drift in driftwood—
a ghost ship with nothing left to bury.

Remembering My Aunt

Our family used to gather for dinner
each Christmas until her husband fell

dead in the driveway one snowy night,
one snowy night that never left her face.

I remember bringing my first camera
to the final meal, Santa's last good idea.

I still have a black and white somewhere,
everyone at the table except me, the only

one alive now, eating at Bruno's alone.
I remember the cheap flash going off

that Christmas, little lights dancing as
they faded in everyone's eyes but mine.

Calling the Children

One day I want to have my children
over, try to explain what happened

to our home years ago. I'll try to touch on
everything they won't remember, finish

the stories that lured them to sleep
aboard the incomplete orbit of a rocker,

recall all the motions that saved them
from the deceptions of endings. I used

to love the postcards of prayer we sent
together, always on our knees, wishing

them away with our eyes open. Always,
the distance between their parents would

accumulate until seasons only arrived
underground—they learned the heat

that warms us springs from our own
fire. I still smell the rain in burnt wood

on nights I can't sleep—just silence now
here with what never happened at home.

With My Daughter Overseas

I've begun to recognize her on this side
as the photographs come sailing over, late
afternoon and an ocean away. From here
everyone looks like a visitor, even locals,
each sample of creation fully immersed

in some unique and unlimited access
to the arts. She visits a castle, discovers
the rotted posts from the fort of herself,
walls she once believed in, partially
died behind as we all must. She stares

at a painting until it's clear she has to
let the painting stare at her if she's to
keep her imaginary brushes dry, allow
the message to mirror a door in her
where nothing's ever been hung. Then

the stories she's heard can settle, a secret
stranger following her from one to another,
someone walking without bones, leaving
her expressions looking unrehearsed
and gracefully afraid. Wine to wine,

she writes home with what won't come
home, can't stay. I've begun to recognize her—
stone peering out of statues, clocks set deep
in steeples, her father always looking out
in wonder at all the water, the late hour.

Calendar

A holiday's here, and secretly
everyone's eyes are lit up
with what's missing—maybe
a grandparent no one's named
after. An aunt? An uncle? We

keep it hid in the rim of each
toast, lie-like, deep in our lips—
by the time we reach ourselves
and the end of the eggnog,
that adolescent lick of rebirth

has gone underground. Serious
talk has drifted to the kitchen,
the dinner prayer playing dead
as the date and time blur into
everyone's version of holiness.

Has the family dog died? God
knows that wasn't on our list
of what not to expect. Funny
how holidays reach into a fire
we look into all our lives, how

they find shadows of what we
never received burning the gifts
we didn't ask for—it's the way
our eyes keep finding the light
and secrets keep coming alive.

The Director at Brookwood School

for my sister

This year's production would be...well,
it doesn't matter yet. The music's involved.
Music's always involved. At this point,
though, it only wants to listen to itself.
The director began in a dark warehouse

of props, her own and the ones with long
shadows, missing covers and anything
that might fit her shaky world of stages.
Recently, cancer had made an appearance,
auditioned a few promises, then asked

to leave, escorted by a few steady hands,
bright lights and the precise dedication
of the dollar. *I'll be around,* it said from
the street. Money was always available
at Brookwood School, which is both good

and bad. To get everything you want
out of song you have to be driven, broke
somewhere inside. And this year, more
than any other, she was. We'll have to
wait and see—her cancer ghost written

deep in the script, the music of opening
night privately tuning the same audience,
the students living out their brief, forever
days, and other props rehearsing the dark
of next year, then the next, and then...

Changes

Alzheimer's was well on its way
to the shapes hiding in the walls
my mother papered with a silence
she couldn't repeat. I finally heard
the prayer my father whispered
when a stroke began to take away
his speech. I've begun to mouth
lessons I learned too late, apologies
I left in mirrors many years ago.
My father never pronounced my
name again until after he died,
and later my mother would gasp
each time I told her I was her son.
It's always been easy for all of us
to feel forgotten. I remember it
being hard to say until now, now
that I can say I never said goodbye.

4

At Mr. Jeff's Music Academy

A little girl on guitar, piano boy, sounds
being urged into the air like dust scaling

some unknown attic draft. Mr. Jeff knows
someday they'll say something, but for now

he leans back and looks through the ceiling,
listens to the children explore the darkness

coming off each lone note, a kind of night
beyond their bed lit up for the first time.

They try their best to move them closer,
sensing the lure of attachments in the air,

some ghostly shapes of tune. But it's no use—
the sharp edges of Mr. Jeff's ears peel away

the dead skin of each attempt. He knows
no matter how many songs they finally fit

on the tip of each finger, one day they'll be
called back, like him, to some single sound;

they'll be forced to lie down in its poor
perfection and die in the dust of a message

only ever sent to themselves. It's something
he must keep from them now, a lesson

only the audience of their own reflection
can teach, and only as they gradually begin

falling into the silence of an empty chair.

Higher Powers

at AA

Another meeting arrives, theoretically
the first, and those of us with less than
nothing to lose gather in a strip store
turned recovery room. On the silent side
of a sealed window, each god goes over
our lines like a good understudy, sure
as dogs certain hungers can't be filled—
take as many steps toward yourself
as you wish, confessions only save
themselves before backing into dark
alleys you've left unlit for years. So,
before it's my turn to testify against
myself, I imagine taking a hammer to
the hairdresser's mirrors, shattering her
saviors into all the selves she's tried
to bleach, a knife to all the dirt beneath
the landscaper's nails, sweeping his holy
ground out the door. My invisible god
knows it's the six-pack's turn to speak,
always on nights I can't make it, nights
like this—the last cigarette of the pack
before burning down all the meetings
I made, the first and, lately, the last.

Passing a Cemetery in Light Rain

By the time it reaches the dead,
drizzle's come together, clouded
congregations of root and coffin,
poured through soil like prayers
gathering in the gutters

of a troubled soul. The usual
heads pop up—parents poking
around apologies, distant relatives
digging dust out of attic mirrors,
me telling a story to myself

too many times. On days like this
I inherit a little more silence,
transplant a few graves
I never covered up. Light
rain illuminates what the sun

can only touch with a moon—
my heaven's hidden in each
stone here. I dream of being
my own forecast, opening
the map of myself, being there.

Psalm

As I sat marinating in thought, gospels falling
from their bones like scales off a mythical fish,

the little prophet in me stood outside his cave
sensing a kind of conversion was close,

a weakness as old as the sky. I felt myself
being pulled into the godlessness of answers,

faith fading into the hands of its own clock.
If what makes sense passes for prayer, some

small salvation was at hand, price reduced
to desire, a guarantee good until saved. When

it came to faith, too much was as weak as not
enough. Having lost interest, the little prophet

returned to his cave disappointed, holding
the bible of himself up against the testament

of stone, burning everything he'd heard
to stay warm. I decided to listen to a sermon

of silence, to follow something that only leads
to itself, something nameless. Like the Magi,

I'd stare at things only I could see. I'd appear
monkish and ready to return some other way.

Common Prayer

After a few short prayers that had
everything to do with me, I noticed
fog lingering beyond sunrise as if

it were asking light if it might stay.
All night it touched everything it
could, running its wet nose over

each flower and trail, its tongue
against every stone and window.
But soon all the colors had arrived

and nothing remembered how close
the fog had come, how clear
it spoke, how it vanished like a star

just as our eyes had finally adjusted
to the absence of answers, the need
for a new arrangement of prayer.

Gospel

"That's what happens when it happens."
—an unknown child

Not something you want
to tell your wife, say, when
you pick a night to announce
you're no longer in love
with her. With children,
however, it's something
you can gingerly turn
to song, have a church
appear in both hands,
complete with people
and steeple and doors
you can control yourself.
Your wife will want to know
more, more than you know
yourself. The only thing
that resembles magic
by then is heartbreak
and its conversion to hate.
Your hands are useless
Your church is empty.
That's what happens,
if it happens. Next time
you're careful about believing
anything that seems to rhyme—
like hymns or sex.

Halloween

for Caleb

I've always wanted to dress up
as someone I secretly wanted to be

all my life—the adulterer, thief, a man
so much like himself people forget his

name, leave him out of stories.
It's the first Halloween I spent

elsewhere in a costume, eating candy
I never bought, waiting at back doors

for a knock only I could hear. I decided
to stay up, try to guess who I was—

I wanted to catch Halloween slipping
out of October and into the clothes

hanging in my closet, headless,
breathing a deep sigh of relief.

In there the dark is always rubbing up
against itself like a strange shadow,

shaping things for some special date,
the chance to hide in plain sight.

Something to Write About

One morning I thought I found it
deep in the vacancy of a ladder.
It had been left leaning oddly
against the steps of my neighbor's
gazebo all night. Other neighbors

spoke softly in the yard, hands
in the air attempting to reenact
something no one witnessed
except those that only alert us
of themselves—cuts in the cedar,

grass bent by the wheels of a stretcher,
a hanging plant growing out of itself,
broken off from the only version
of earth it knew. I've longed for this
kind of occurrence to write about,

to make me feel alive again. I'd been
lost in my own history of change,
condemned by alternate outcomes,
so deep in the silence of my own
stories even the siren that shadowed

my neighbor away couldn't wake me.
I needed the guilt that was slowly
stirring its invisible ink—the path
just being a path, this morning
another moment just out of reach.

Listening to Grackles

Always complaining, especially when
one stabs a handout. No hiding. Dogfights

flare and, one by one, the crumbs drop into
the marsh where shiners extend the frenzy

to their world of silence. Scattered insults
now, darkness dropping its own net over

the bayou. The owl, the hawk, and the hunt
study the landscape in separate trees. And

there I am, walking away through my life,
pushing off, still deciding on a new plan.

Picture

Two hawks high on the dead
branches of a cedar, in the distance

thunderheads in bloom, and between
it all a half-rainbow getting fat off

bogs and wetlands where mosquitoes
make their plans. The air's about

to be charged; nitrogen knows
just where to go, what to touch.

It's as close as promises can come
without turning to luck. Even the all-

telling tech of weathermen can't
account for the motions of a man.

I've lost everything on a day so clear...
held the healing power of postponements,

slept with the snowbound where
all the white in the world won't add up

to a clear answer. The hawk's black eyes
are out of sight but know exactly when

each one of my muscles move, even
my heart—especially my heart—

that sparrow or squirrel living on
what's not enough, a synergist

lust-lined, out of focus, always
too many steps away from home.

Light and Dark During the Sermon

Then there's how light passes through
the apostle's face on the stained glass
window, especially his eyes. What

does he see now that we know? His lips...
what would he say if he knew? The priest
announces someone's burial. The offering

is next, that gray area where gods have
room to work. A few pews of poor souls
feel it getting late for all their own reasons.

Midwest of His Mind

He longs for the loose sand again, footprints
that can only be followed so far, one more
chance to follow them. In dreams he's the ship,
the bottle, the wind picking up inside—he loves
the certainty of a good compass, the way

destinations drop off like time and distance.
He's never lost his deep passion for changing
tides, the give and take of a faceless moon.
At the end of the day he hopes he's far enough
from home to feel at home with all the vague

expressions embedded in the beach like fists
in a pillow. For him there's something about
the sound of shells coming together at night,
wave after wave, horizons placing themselves
between what he loves and what he longs for.

Acknowledgments

I am grateful to the following magazines in which many of these poems first appeared, sometimes in a different form.

Carolina Quarterly: "Waking Up Asleep"
Dialogist: "Lightning and Love"
Flare: "Roads"
Hawaii Pacific Review: "Headlights"
Kentucky Review: "Calling," "With My Daughter Overseas"
Lindenwood Review: "Night Light," "Light and Dark During
    the Sermon"
Philadelphia Stories: "Stone"
Pirene's Fountain: "Shelling," "Remembering My Aunt,"
    "Passing a Cemetery in Light Rain"
Prick of the Spindle: "At Oyster Point," "Salt Love"
Red Earth Review: "Picture," "Dog Homeless and Down"
Scapegoat Review: "Impatient at Diana's Salon"
Split Rock Review: "Return Address"

*Cover background photo, "Origami Illumination" by
Paul Stevenson; author photo by Kate Bishop; cover and interior
book design by Diane Kistner; Georgia text and Haboro Bold
Condensed titling*

About FutureCycle Press

FutureCycle Press is dedicated to publishing lasting English-language poetry books, chapbooks, and anthologies in both print-on-demand and Kindle ebook formats. Founded in 2007 by long-time independent editor/publishers and partners Diane Kistner and Robert S. King, the press incorporated as a nonprofit in 2012. A number of our editors are distinguished poets and writers in their own right, and we have been actively involved in the small press movement going back to the early seventies.

The FutureCycle Poetry Book Prize and honorarium is awarded annually for the best full-length volume of poetry we publish in a calendar year. Introduced in 2013, our Good Works projects are anthologies devoted to issues of universal significance, with all proceeds donated to a related worthy cause. Our Selected Poems series highlights contemporary poets with a substantial body of work to their credit; with this series we strive to resurrect work that has had limited distribution and is now out of print.

We are dedicated to giving all of the authors we publish the care their work deserves, making our catalog of titles the most diverse and distinguished it can be, and paying forward any earnings to fund more great books.

We've learned a few things about independent publishing over the years. We've also evolved a unique, resilient publishing model that allows us to focus mainly on vetting and preserving for posterity poetry collections of exceptional quality without becoming overwhelmed with bookkeeping and mailing, fundraising activities, or taxing editorial and production "bubbles." To find out more about what we are doing, come see us at www.futurecycle.org.

The FutureCycle Poetry Book Prize

All full-length volumes of poetry published by FutureCycle Press in a given calendar year are considered for the annual FutureCycle Poetry Book Prize. This allows us to consider each submission on its own merits, outside of the context of a contest. Too, the judges see the finished book, which will have benefitted from the beautiful book design and strong editorial gloss we are famous for.

The book ranked the best in judging is announced as the prize-winner in the subsequent year. There is no fixed monetary award; instead, the winning poet receives an honorarium of 20% of the total net royalties from all poetry books and chapbooks the press sold online in the year the winning book was published. The winner is also accorded the honor of being on the panel of judges for the next year's competition; all judges receive copies of all contending books to keep for their personal library.

CPSIA information can be obtained
at www.ICGtesting.com
Printed in the USA
FFHW011743210119
50261511-55252FF